Volatile Markets

Jackson Brooks

Index

Introduction to Market Volatility

Volatility is one of those terms that, although it sounds technical, is essential for anyone who wants to get into the world of trading. Imagine that you are on a roller coaster, where the ups and downs are unpredictable, and although the ride can be exciting, it can also be terrifying if you don't know what's coming. This is volatility in financial markets: those moments of instability and rapid changes in prices that can make an asset go from being at the top to plummeting in a matter of minutes, or vice versa.

When we talk about volatility in a market, we are referring to the magnitude and frequency of changes in the prices of assets such as stocks, bonds, currencies or cryptocurrencies. A volatile market is one where prices rise and fall significantly in short periods of time. For the trader, this means both risks and opportunities. In a stable market, price movements are more predictable and usually slower; in a volatile market, however, everything can change at any moment.

Volatility can be triggered by a variety of factors. Economic news, changes in government policies, central bank decisions, or even unexpected events such as a pandemic are all elements that can increase or decrease volatility. For example, an announcement about new financial regulation or the outcome of a major election can trigger an instant reaction in the market, causing asset prices to fluctuate rapidly. And sometimes, no external event is necessary: the very behavior of investors, guided by fear or greed, can cause prices to rise or fall dramatically.

For traders, volatility is a phenomenon that can seem scary, but it is also the source of great opportunities. When prices move quickly, there is the potential for huge profits if you can correctly anticipate those movements. Imagine that you buy a stock at a low price and, due to market volatility, its price skyrockets within a few hours. You can sell it and make a significant profit in a very short time. But, as with everything, there is a downside to this scenario. Volatility can also work against you. Just as the price of an asset can rise quickly, it can also plummet, generating considerable losses if the risks are not managed properly.

It is important to remember that volatility is neither good nor bad in itself. It all depends on how you handle it. For experienced traders, a volatile market can be a goldmine if they know how to navigate it. However, for those who are new to the game, volatility can be overwhelming and dangerous if precautions are not taken. Rapid market movements can cause even the calmest of traders to panic or get carried away by excitement, making impulsive decisions that could lead to losses.

One fascinating aspect of volatility is that it is not always the same. There are periods when markets are relatively calm, with few significant changes in prices, and other times when everything seems to be in constant motion. This difference is due, in part, to the fact that volatility follows cycles. During certain periods, the market may be more stable, while in other periods, whether due to the accumulation of internal or external factors, prices can become unpredictable. This cyclical behavior is what causes some traders to adopt specific strategies for volatile markets and others for when the market is calmer.

As we delve deeper into the topic of volatility in the following chapters, we will see that there are ways to measure it, analyze it, and even take advantage of it. Not everything is chaos. There are tools and strategies that allow traders to make informed decisions, based on patterns and careful analysis. Volatility, while unpredictable in nature, has its rules, and learning to understand them is key for anyone who wants to trade in these markets.

In short, volatility is the element that adds dynamism to markets. It is the pulse that makes prices rise and fall, sometimes unpredictably, and it is what allows the most skilled traders to find opportunities amidst uncertainty. But it is also a reminder that trading in financial markets is not just about quick profits, but about understanding the risks and knowing when is the right time to enter or exit. And that balance, between taking advantage of volatility and protecting yourself from it, is what separates successful traders from those who only chase the thrill of the moment.

Identifying Volatile Markets

Identifying a volatile market is like trying to predict when a storm is about to break. It doesn't just happen out of nowhere, there are always signs that anticipate it, and learning to read those signs is key for any trader who wants to successfully navigate these turbulent waters. Volatility in the markets doesn't arise from a single factor, but from a combination of elements that together form an unpredictable environment, where prices can move sharply up or down. In this chapter, we will see how to identify these volatile markets clearly and easily.

The first step to recognizing a volatile market is to pay attention to unusual price movements. If you notice that an asset, whether it's a stock, cryptocurrency, or currency, starts to have more pronounced fluctuations than usual, that's a clear sign of volatility. For example, if a stock that normally fluctuates in price by 1% a day suddenly starts to swing by 5% or more, that's a warning that something is up. These wild movements can be caused by a variety of reasons, from economic news to changes in policy or even just the collective behavior of investors.

Another important indicator for spotting volatile markets is trading volume. Volume refers to the amount of trading that takes place in a market over a given period. When volume increases significantly, it usually means that something is attracting investors' attention, which in turn can lead to an increase in volatility. Think of volume as the noise level in a room. If volume is high, it's like there are a lot of people talking at the same time, indicating that something important is happening. In markets, when a lot of people are buying and selling frantically, prices tend to move more quickly, creating a more volatile environment.

Economic and political events also play a crucial role in identifying volatile markets. Announcements such as interest rate decisions by central banks, earnings reports by large companies, or even unexpected events such as an international crisis, can trigger volatility in markets. For example, when a company announces results that are much better or worse than expected, its stock prices can react violently, rising or falling rapidly. Similarly, a decision by a central bank to raise or lower interest rates can generate abrupt movements in financial markets, especially in the currency and bond markets.

A very useful tool for identifying volatility in the markets is the volatility index, also known as the VIX. The VIX measures expectations of volatility in the stock market and is often referred to as the "fear index." When the VIX rises, it generally means that investors are anticipating sharper price movements and, therefore, greater volatility. The VIX can be an excellent barometer for assessing whether a market is entering a phase of instability or whether, on the contrary, prices are expected to remain more stable.

Another thing to look for is sudden trends on price charts. Technical patterns can offer clues as to when a market is becoming volatile. For example, if you notice that an asset's prices are forming sharp peaks and troughs over a short period of time, that indicates that prices are not following a stable pattern and that volatility is increasing. Technical traders often use tools like Bollinger Bands, which measure volatility by looking at how prices are expanding or contracting around a moving average. If the bands are widening, that's a sign that volatility is increasing.

Volatile markets also tend to have more "gaps," which are spaces on charts where the price of an asset jumps sharply from one level to another without passing through the intermediate values. Gaps often appear after important events or at the opening of markets, when news or announcements made outside of trading hours cause an instant reaction in prices. If an asset has a lot of gaps, especially up and down, you are likely in a volatile environment.

Finally, it is important to be aware of market behavior during times of uncertainty or panic. Financial markets, like people, overreact to fear and uncertainty. When investors are unsure of what will happen, they tend to make impulsive decisions, which increases volatility. During these periods, markets can move in opposite directions abruptly, and prices can fluctuate for no apparent reason. This type of irrational behavior is another indicator that the market has become volatile.

In short, identifying volatile markets requires a combination of careful observation and the use of key tools. Sharp price movements, increased trading volume, economic and political events, and technical indicators such as the VIX or Bollinger Bands are all factors that will help you detect when a market is entering a phase of high volatility. Knowing how to recognize these signs is essential for any trader, as it will allow you to anticipate changes, adjust your strategies, and, above all, protect yourself from the risks that come with trading in unstable environments. The key is to always be alert, observe the patterns, and not get carried away by emotions, because in volatile markets, success lies in being one step ahead of the chaos.

Opportunities in Volatility

When we hear the word "volatility," many automatically think of risk, chaos, and danger. And it's true that volatile markets can be tricky and risky, but it's also important to understand that amidst all that turbulence, there are opportunities waiting to be seized. In fact, for many traders, volatility is the perfect setting to make big moves and make significant profits. So how is it possible to see opportunity in an environment that seems so uncertain? The key is to understand that rapid price movements can be both an advantage and a disadvantage, depending on how you handle them.

Volatility creates opportunities because when prices change sharply in a short period of time, there is a chance to buy an asset at a low price and sell it quickly at a higher price. Think of it like the ups and downs of a roller coaster. If you can get on the bandwagon at the right time, just before the rise begins, you can enjoy a big profit when you reach the top. In financial markets, this means that if you have the ability to predict, or at least intuit, when an asset is going to rise or fall significantly, you can take advantage of those fluctuations to increase your profits.

One of the biggest appeals of volatile markets is that they offer the potential to make profits over much shorter time frames than in more stable markets. In a stable market, prices tend to move slowly, and traders often have to wait days, weeks, or even months for a trade to yield a noticeable return. In a volatile market, however, those moves can happen in a matter of minutes or hours. This speed can be incredibly exciting and lucrative for those who know how to move quickly and make decisions based on analysis of market movements.

Trading strategies designed specifically for volatile markets often focus on capturing these quick profit opportunities. For example, day trading and swing trading are two popular approaches that seek to take advantage of short-term movements in volatile markets. Day trading involves buying and selling assets on the same day, taking advantage of price fluctuations that occur during market hours. In volatile markets, this approach can be particularly effective, as prices can move considerably over the course of a single session. Swing trading, on the other hand, involves holding a position for a few days or weeks, attempting to capture the wider swings that result from short- and medium-term volatility.

Another aspect that makes volatile markets attractive is the ability to profit from both up and down moves. In stable markets, most traders tend to focus on buying low and selling high. However, in a volatile market, you can not only profit when prices rise, but also when they fall. This is achieved through strategies such as short selling, which allows traders to profit when the price of an asset falls. Essentially, you are selling an asset that you do not own, hoping to buy it back later at a lower price and pocket the difference. In volatile markets, where falls can be as rapid and steep as rises, this strategy can be a powerful tool for generating profits even in the midst of chaos.

Furthermore, volatility can open up opportunities in assets that would not normally attract attention. When a market becomes volatile, it is not just the big players such as technology stocks or the currency market that experience changes. Less popular assets such as certain commodities or smaller company stocks can also be affected and present unique opportunities. Traders who stay alert and diversify their portfolios can find little hidden gems in these little-known assets that, thanks to volatility, can generate unexpected returns.

Another interesting aspect is that volatility tends to attract more participants to the market, which in turn can further amplify opportunities. When a market is stable, some traders and investors may be indifferent, waiting for better times to act. But as soon as volatility spikes, many enter the game, creating more liquidity and opportunities for those who are prepared. This increased activity can also generate more information and patterns to follow, making it easier to analyze the market to make more informed decisions.

However, while opportunities in volatile markets can be tempting, it is crucial to remember that not all fluctuations are easy to predict or take advantage of. Volatile markets can be incredibly unpredictable, and price movements that appear to indicate a clear trend can reverse at any time. This is where risk management comes into play. To capitalize on opportunities in a volatile market, it is essential to have a solid strategy in place to limit potential losses. This includes the use of stop-loss orders, which allow a trade to be closed automatically if the price of an asset falls below a predetermined level, and diversification, which helps spread risk across multiple assets.

In short, volatile markets offer a wealth of opportunities for those traders willing to take the associated risks. Rapid price movements, the possibility of profiting on both ups and downs, and the ability to find undervalued assets are just a few of the advantages that can make volatility appealing. But as always, success in these markets depends on having a well-thought-out strategy, staying informed, and not getting carried away by the emotion of the moment. If you can master the art of trading volatile markets, the rewards can be immense, but only if you know how to take advantage of each opportunity with caution and precision.

Risks Associated with Volatility

Volatility, while it can offer great opportunities for traders, also comes with a number of risks that should not be taken lightly. In fact, for many investors, the risks associated with volatility are the main reason they prefer to stay away from these volatile markets. When asset prices move quickly and unpredictably, the potential for quick profits goes hand in hand with the possibility of losing money just as quickly. It's like walking a tightrope: the rewards can be great if you make it to the other side, but the risk of falling is always present.

One of the biggest risks in volatile markets is the possibility of suffering large losses in a very short period of time. In a relatively stable market, price changes are usually gradual, giving traders time to react and adjust their positions. However, in a volatile market, prices can move so sharply that before you know it, you may be facing a considerable loss. Imagine that you have bought shares in a company expecting them to rise, but suddenly, due to unexpected news, the price plummets in a matter of minutes. If you do not act quickly, you could lose a large portion of your investment in the blink of an eye.

Another common risk is market "noise." In a volatile environment, asset prices can move randomly, without following clear patterns. This can make it extremely difficult for traders to make informed decisions. Often, sudden price movements have no apparent cause and can simply be motivated by panic or the excitement of other investors. This type of chaotic behavior can lead to rash decisions, such as buying or selling based on a false alarm, which in turn can result in significant losses. In short, volatile markets are prone to creating distractions and misleading movements, which can lead traders to make poor decisions.

Volatility can also increase the risk of overexposure. In their eagerness to take advantage of rapid price fluctuations, some traders may be tempted to risk more capital than they should. The problem is that in a volatile market, even seemingly safe trades can suddenly turn against you. If a trader puts too much money into a single trade expecting a big profit, and the market unexpectedly changes direction, the losses can be devastating. This type of overexposure can cause a single mistake or unexpected move to wipe out weeks or months of profits.

Volatility also tends to increase the use of leverage, which can be both a powerful tool and a double-edged sword. Leverage allows traders to trade with more money than they actually have, increasing both the potential for profit and loss. In a stable market, leverage can be a useful way to increase returns. However, in a volatile market, where prices can move sharply in both directions, leverage can become a dangerous trap. If prices move against your position, you could lose more than you originally invested, which could lead to considerable debt or even bankruptcy in extreme cases.

Another risk to consider in volatile markets is the emotional impact. Volatility can create an environment of constant stress and pressure, which can lead traders to act impulsively or emotionally. When prices rise and fall rapidly, it is easy to get carried away by panic or greed, often resulting in irrational decisions. For example, a trader may see an investment rapidly lose value and, in fear, sell at a low price only to see the market recover shortly after. Similarly, a trader who sees his assets rise rapidly may become overconfident and risk more capital than necessary, only to see the market turn against him unexpectedly. Emotional control is crucial in a volatile environment, and a lack of this control can greatly amplify risks.

Additionally, in volatile markets, there is a risk of getting stuck in an illiquid position. When prices move quickly, especially in less liquid assets, it can be difficult to find buyers or sellers willing to execute your trade at the desired price. This can mean that even if you want to exit a position to limit your losses, you may not find anyone willing to buy your assets, leaving you stuck in a losing situation without being able to react. Lack of liquidity can greatly increase losses in a volatile market, as you won't always have the option to exit when you need to most.

Spread widening is also a major risk in volatile markets. The spread is the difference between the buy price and the sell price of an asset. In times of stability, spreads tend to be relatively small, making it easier to enter and exit positions. However, in times of high volatility, spreads can widen dramatically, meaning you could pay a higher price when buying and receive a lower price when selling. This can increase transaction costs and reduce profits, or even turn a seemingly profitable trade into a loss-making one.

Last but not least, there is the risk of incorrect or outdated information. In a volatile market, news and relevant information move quickly, and traders who do not have access to the most up-to-date information may make decisions based on outdated data. In an environment where prices can change in a matter of seconds, trading on outdated information can lead to significant losses. Furthermore, in times of high volatility, rumors and misinformation tend to circulate more frequently, which can confuse traders and lead them to act incorrectly.

In summary, while volatility offers many opportunities, it is also fraught with considerable risks. Large losses in short periods of time, market noise, overexposure, improper use of leverage, lack of emotional control, lack of liquidity, widening spreads and incorrect information are all factors that can work against a trader in volatile markets. The key to successfully trading in these environments is to recognize these risks, have a clear plan to manage them and, above all, not get carried away by panic or euphoria of the moment. Only in this way can a balance be found between taking advantage of opportunities and protecting oneself from the dangers that accompany volatility.

Techniques for Trading in Volatile Markets

Trading in volatile markets requires not only great skill and knowledge, but also a clear and well-defined strategy. In such environments, where asset prices can move rapidly and unpredictably, it is essential to have techniques that allow traders to protect their capital while taking advantage of the opportunities that arise from volatility. There are various techniques that traders can employ to successfully navigate these unstable markets. Some of these techniques focus on risk management, while others focus on how to maximize potential profits. Here I will explain some of the most effective ones.

One of the most basic and fundamental techniques for trading in volatile markets is proper risk management. This involves, first of all, not putting more money on the line than you are willing to lose. While this seems like a simple rule, it is surprising how many traders forget it when they see the possibility of making huge profits in a market that is going up and down rapidly. The general rule of thumb is to not risk more than 1% to 2% of your total capital on a single trade. This way, even if things don't go your way, you will be able to absorb the losses without them drastically affecting your account. Risk management is not only about limiting losses, but also about making sure that you can continue trading in the long term.

Another important technique is the use of stop-loss orders. In a volatile market, prices can change direction in a matter of seconds, and if you don't have a plan to limit your losses, you could end up losing more money than you thought. A stop-loss order is a tool that allows you to set a price at which your position will automatically close if the market moves against you. For example, if you buy a stock at $100, you could set a stop-loss at $95. If the price falls to that level, your position will automatically be sold, limiting your losses to just $5 per share. In volatile markets, where sharp moves are common, stop-loss orders can be a lifesaver.

In addition to stop-loss orders, some traders also use take-profit orders, which work in the opposite way. While stop-loss orders close your position if the price falls too far, take-profit orders do so if the price rises enough to secure a profit. This is useful in volatile markets, as it prevents you from staying too long in a winning position that could quickly reverse. For example, if you buy a stock at $100 and set a take-profit at $110, your position will automatically close when the price reaches that level, guaranteeing a $10 profit per share before the market can turn against you.

Another technique commonly used in volatile markets is portfolio diversification. Instead of putting all your money into one asset or sector, diversification involves spreading your capital across different types of assets. This can include stocks, bonds, currencies, commodities, and even cryptocurrencies. By doing so, you reduce the risk of suffering large losses if a single asset or market becomes extremely volatile. The idea behind diversification is that if one asset is down, another may be up, which helps balance your portfolio and protect you from extreme market movements.

Margin trading is another technique that some traders use to trade volatile markets, but it comes with a lot of risk. Margin allows you to borrow money to trade, which amplifies both your profits and losses. While this technique can be extremely profitable in volatile markets, it can also lead to huge losses if the market moves against you. For this reason, margin trading should only be used by experienced traders who have a solid understanding of the risks involved. In a volatile market, it's easy to get caught up in rapid moves that can wipe out a leveraged account in a matter of minutes.

Technical analysis is another very valuable technique for trading in volatile markets. This approach involves using charts, patterns, and other indicators to predict how prices will move in the future. Some of the most commonly used technical indicators in volatile markets include Bollinger Bands, the Relative Strength Index (RSI), and moving averages. Bollinger Bands, for example, measure market volatility by showing the distance between an asset's current price and its moving average. When the bands widen, it means volatility is increasing, which can be a sign that major moves are coming. Traders can use this type of information to decide when to enter or exit a trade.

Analysis of news and macroeconomic events is also crucial in volatile markets. Large price movements are often triggered by unexpected news, such as economic reports, changes in government policy, or global events, such as natural disasters or political crises. Staying on top of current news and events can help you anticipate volatility and adjust your trading accordingly. For example, if you know that a key economic report is coming out soon, you might choose not to trade at that time to avoid the associated volatility. Or, you might take the opportunity to trade based on the results of the report.

Patience is another essential technique for trading in volatile markets. While it can be tempting to jump on every price move, it is often better to wait for the market to give you a clear signal before acting. In a volatile environment, price movements can be erratic and misleading, and acting on impulse can lead to poor decisions. Waiting for a trend to be confirmed before entering a trade can help you avoid many market pitfalls. Remember that you don't always have to be trading. Sometimes, the best strategy is to simply observe and wait for the right moment to act.

Another technique is to reduce your position size when the market becomes more volatile than usual. Instead of trading with large sums of money, trading with smaller positions can help you reduce risk and better handle market fluctuations. This is especially useful in extremely volatile markets, where price movements can be unpredictable and rapid. By reducing your position size, you limit your exposure and give yourself more room to maneuver in case things don't go as you expected.

Finally, one of the most important techniques for trading in volatile markets is to stay calm and not get carried away by emotions. Volatility can trigger both fear and euphoria, and it's easy to make impulsive decisions when prices are rising or falling rapidly. However, acting on emotion rather than relying on a solid strategy is a recipe for disaster. It's crucial that you stay disciplined and stick to your trading plan, even when the market seems to be moving against you. Remember that volatility is part of the game, and successful traders are those who know how to hold their ground amidst the chaos.

In short, trading in volatile markets requires a combination of well-thought-out techniques and discipline. From risk management and the use of stop-loss orders, to technical analysis and portfolio diversification, there are many tools at the disposal of traders looking to take advantage of volatility without being overtaken by it. Although these markets can be difficult to navigate, with the right strategy and a rational approach, it is possible to not only survive, but thrive amidst volatility.

Risk Management in Unstable Markets

Risk management is perhaps the most important part of trading in volatile markets. In an environment where prices can rise and fall unexpectedly, the risk of losing money increases considerably. No matter how experienced a trader you are, or how well you think you understand the market, if you don't have a solid strategy for managing risk, you are exposed to significant losses. The goal of risk management is not to avoid risk altogether, as that is impossible in trading, but to ensure that you can limit losses and continue trading in the long term.

The first thing you need to do when it comes to managing risk is to set a clear limit for how much you are willing to lose on each trade. This is a basic principle, but it is something that many traders overlook, especially when things seem to be going well or when they think they can "win back" their losses. The general rule of thumb that many successful traders use is to not risk more than 1% to 2% of your capital on any one trade. This means that even if a trade goes completely against you, your losses will be small enough that they will not drastically affect your account. For example, if you have an account with $10,000, you should not risk more than $100 to $200 on a single trade. This way, if you have a losing streak, you will still have enough capital to keep trading and recover.

Another essential technique for risk management in volatile markets is the use of stop-loss orders. A stop-loss is a tool that allows you to set an automatic limit on how much you are willing to lose on a trade. If the market moves against you and hits the price you have set as your stop-loss, your position will be closed automatically. This is crucial in volatile markets, where prices can move quickly and you won't always have the opportunity to close a trade manually. The stop-loss acts as a safety net, protecting you from losses greater than you are willing to take. The key to using stop-losses effectively is to place them at strategic points, far enough away from the current price to give the market room to fluctuate, but not so far away as to allow significant losses.

In addition to stop-loss orders, some people use take-profit orders as part of their risk management strategy. While stop-loss orders focus on limiting losses, take-profit orders focus on securing profits before the market can turn against you. In an unstable market, prices can change direction quickly, and it can be tempting to sit on a winning trade hoping for more profits. However, this can also be risky, as an unrealized profit can quickly disappear if the market changes course. By setting a take-profit level, you ensure that when the price reaches a favorable point, your trade will automatically close, guaranteeing a profit no matter what happens next. This technique can help you maintain a disciplined approach, avoiding the risk of getting too greedy.

Another key part of risk management is diversification. Diversification involves not putting all of your money into one asset or market. Instead of concentrating your capital on one trade, you spread your money across different assets or market types. This can include stocks, currencies, commodities, or even cryptocurrencies. The goal of diversification is to reduce the risk of large losses if a single market or asset experiences extreme volatility. For example, if you invest all of your capital in technology stocks and that sector suffers a sudden crash, you could lose a large portion of your money. However, if you have a diversified portfolio that includes technology stocks, bonds, currencies, and commodities, losses in one area can be offset by gains in others. Diversification is like a cushion that softens market shocks, spreading risk rather than concentrating it.

Reducing position sizes is another effective risk management strategy in volatile markets. When the market becomes extremely volatile, it is a good practice to reduce the amount of money you put into each trade. This allows you to limit the impact of any sudden market movements. For example, if you normally invest $10,000 into a trade, you could reduce that amount to $5,000 or even less during periods of high volatility. This way, if the market moves against you, your losses will be smaller. This technique is particularly useful when the market shows unpredictable movements and it is not clear where it will go. By trading smaller positions, you give yourself more room to maneuver and reduce the overall risk in your account.

Using leverage is a double-edged sword in volatile markets. Leverage allows you to trade with more money than you actually have, which can amplify both your profits and losses. In stable markets, leverage can be a useful tool to increase your returns. However, in volatile markets, leverage can significantly increase the risk of large losses. If the market moves against you, you could lose more than you have invested, and this can lead to a rapid financial collapse. For this reason, it is advisable to reduce the use of leverage during periods of high volatility, or eliminate it altogether if you are not completely sure how to handle it. Prudence is key when it comes to leverage in volatile markets.

Emotional control is also an essential part of risk management in these environments. Volatile markets can create an emotional roller coaster, with constant ups and downs that can cause traders to make rash decisions. Fear and greed are emotions that, if not managed properly, can lead to poor decisions. For example, fear can cause you to close a losing position too early, while greed can cause you to hold on to a winning position for too long, only to see the market turn against you. The key to managing these emotions is to have a clear plan and stick to it, no matter what is happening in the market. By having a defined strategy, you can avoid making impulsive decisions based on momentary emotions.

Another effective risk management technique is to stay informed about the factors that can influence market volatility. Macroeconomic events, political decisions, and important news can have a significant impact on the markets. Staying abreast of key economic events and news can help you anticipate market movements and adjust your trading accordingly. For example, if you know that an important economic report is coming out in the next few days, you might choose not to trade or reduce your position sizes to avoid the volatility that could arise after the report. Preparation and anticipation are essential to effectively managing risk in volatile markets.

Finally, a key strategy in risk management is knowing when not to trade. In extremely volatile markets, sometimes the best option is to simply sit on the sidelines and wait for conditions to improve. Many traders feel the need to be constantly in the market, but trading in highly volatile conditions without a clear strategy can do more harm than good. Taking a breath and calmly analyzing the market can give you a clearer perspective and prevent you from making impulsive decisions. Knowing when not to trade is just as important as knowing when to trade.

In short, risk management in volatile markets is critical for any trader who wants to survive and thrive in these environments. From setting clear loss limits and using stop-loss orders, to diversifying your portfolio and managing your emotions, there are a variety of techniques you can use to protect your capital. While volatility can offer exciting opportunities, it also comes with considerable risks, and the key to success is ensuring those risks are controlled. By implementing effective risk management, you can navigate volatile markets with greater confidence and minimize losses, ensuring you'll be well-positioned to take advantage of opportunities when they arise.

Psychology of Trading in Volatile Markets

Trading psychology is a fundamental aspect of being successful in the financial markets, and when it comes to trading in volatile markets, its importance is magnified even more. Volatility, with its rapid price changes and unexpected movements, can trigger an emotional roller coaster for any trader, from the most novice to the most experienced. Staying calm, making rational decisions, and preventing emotions from controlling our actions is a constant challenge. In this chapter, we are going to explore how psychology plays a key role in volatile markets and how you can train your mind to better navigate these uncertain environments.

One of the biggest psychological challenges in trading volatile markets is fear. Fear is a natural emotion that all humans experience, and when it comes to money, that fear can be heightened. In volatile markets, where prices can drop sharply in a matter of minutes, the fear of losing money can lead to rash and irrational decisions. For example, you might close a trade at a loss just because you fear the market will continue to fall, without considering whether there are fundamentals to support that decision. Fear can cause you to exit a trade too soon, missing the opportunity for the market to recover and for you to make a profit.

On the other hand, there is greed. Greed is the counterpart to fear and can also be extremely detrimental in volatile markets. In the midst of rapid bullish moves, it is easy to feel euphoric and think that prices will continue to rise endlessly. This emotion can lead many traders to hold winning positions for too long, hoping for more profits, only to see the market suddenly reverse and those profits wiped out. Greed leads you to take unnecessary risks, over-leverage yourself, or ignore clear signals that you should exit a trade. Controlling greed is essential to maintaining discipline and not getting carried away by impulses.

Trading in volatile markets can also lead to what is known as "analysis paralysis." This term refers to the inability to make decisions due to information overload. In a highly volatile environment, traders are often faced with a flood of data, charts, and news that can be overwhelming. The more volatile the market, the harder it becomes to process all of that information effectively. Analysis paralysis can cause you to miss out on valuable opportunities simply because you can't decide whether to enter or exit a trade. The fear of making a mistake or making the wrong decision can cause you to sit still, taking no action, while the market continues to move.

One of the most common psychological mistakes in volatile markets is the need to "get back" at the market after a loss. This behavior is dangerous because it leads to making impulsive and ill-considered decisions, with the goal of quickly recovering what was lost. Imagine that you have had a bad trade and lost money; the immediate instinct might be to quickly open another trade to try to recover what you lost. However, revenge trading often leads to irrational decisions and, in most cases, to further losses. In volatile markets, where movements can be unpredictable, this type of impulsiveness is especially dangerous.

To handle trading psychology in volatile markets, it is crucial to develop a mindset based on discipline and patience. Discipline is what will allow you to stick to your trading plan, even when the market is choppy and emotions are running high. Part of that discipline involves having a clear plan before entering any trade: knowing how much you are willing to lose, how much you expect to win, and when you will exit, no matter what is happening in the market at the time. A disciplined trader does not panic or euphoria; he simply follows his strategy, trusting that in the long run, the well-structured plan will yield positive results.

Patience is another key virtue when, trading volatile markets. During times of high volatility, it's easy to feel anxious about entering a trade to take advantage of rapid market movements. However, it's often better to wait for clear signals to present themselves before acting. Patience allows you to avoid making impulsive decisions and helps you stay calm amidst uncertainty. Many traders believe that they must constantly trade to make money, but in reality, sometimes the best decision is to do nothing and wait for market conditions to become more favorable.

Another important aspect of trading psychology in volatile markets is accepting that losses are part of the game. In any type of trading, losses are inevitable, but in volatile markets, where sharp price swings are more common, losses can be more frequent. Accepting this up front will allow you to better deal with the negative emotions that come with a failed trade. Instead of obsessing over every loss, you should learn to view it as a natural part of the process. The important thing is that your gains, over time, outweigh your losses. Developing a mindset where you accept losses will allow you to continue trading without carrying the emotional weight of a losing streak.

Emotional self-control is another pillar of trading psychology. The market has no emotions, but traders do, and it is very easy to be influenced by what is happening in real time. If you allow emotions to control you, you are likely to make poor decisions. To avoid this, it is important to have practices that help you stay calm and focused. Some traders find it helpful to practice meditation or breathing exercises to relax and reduce stress. Others prefer to take small breaks throughout the day to clear their minds and prevent accumulated stress from affecting their decisions. The most important thing is to find what works for you and helps you maintain a calm mindset.

An effective psychological approach in volatile markets is to think of trading as a marathon, not a sprint. Successful traders understand that success isn't about winning on every trade, but rather about building a consistent track record over time. In volatile markets, where price changes can be dramatic, it's easy to feel pressured to get quick results. However, keeping a long-term perspective will help you avoid making hasty decisions and keep your cool when the market doesn't behave the way you expected. Having a long-term mindset also allows you to look past short-term losses and focus on your overall success as a trader.

Another useful psychological tool in volatile markets is confidence in yourself and your trading plan. During times of high volatility, it's easy to doubt yourself and your decisions, especially if the market is against you. However, self-doubt can be paralyzing and lead to impulsive decisions. If you've done your research, if you've developed a solid strategy and have a clear plan, it's important to trust that. Confidence doesn't mean being arrogant or ignoring market signals, but rather believing in your ability to make well-informed decisions. That confidence will allow you to stay calm even in the most turbulent times.

Finally, it's crucial to have a support system. Trading can be a lonely business, and in times of extreme volatility, it's easy to feel isolated. Talking to other traders, sharing experiences, and learning from others can be a huge help in maintaining emotional balance. Whether through forums, social media, or trading groups, having a community you can discuss your trades and emotions with will give you a broader perspective and reduce the pressure of making decisions alone. Additionally, hearing about others' experiences can help you learn new strategies and ways to handle volatility from an emotional standpoint.

In conclusion, trading psychology in volatile markets is a determining factor for success. Emotions such as fear and greed can negatively influence your decisions, but with discipline, patience, emotional control, and a long-term mindset, you can navigate these markets more effectively. Accepting losses, trusting your plan, and surrounding yourself with a supportive community will allow you to stay calm even when the market is at its most unstable. Remember that trading is not only about technical skills, but also about the ability to control your mind in the most challenging situations.

When to Leave a Volatile Market

Knowing when to exit a volatile market is one of the most difficult, but also most crucial, decisions a trader must face. Often, the temptation to continue trading in a choppy market can be great, either out of hope that the situation will improve or out of fear of missing out on a potential opportunity. However, volatile markets do not always offer favorable conditions, and in many cases, staying in too long can result in big losses. In this chapter, we are going to explore the key moments when you should consider exiting a volatile market and the signs that indicate it is time to take a step back.

The first sign that it's time to exit a volatile market is when the volatility begins to overwhelm your ability to emotionally handle it. Volatile markets create rapid and sometimes violent swings in prices, which can increase stress and anxiety for any trader. If you find yourself trading in fear or feeling overwhelmed by how quickly prices are changing, it's a sign that it may be time to stop. Trading under emotional pressure rarely results in rational decisions. If you notice that your emotions are influencing your trading, or if you're tempted to make impulsive moves, it's best to take a break and exit the market until you regain control of your emotions.

Another time to consider exiting a volatile market is when you realize that you are trading without a clear plan. Volatility can cause you to get carried away by the immediacy of the moves and forget about your original strategy. If you find yourself entering and exiting trades without proper analysis, simply going with the flow of the market, you are likely making decisions based on short-termism, which increases the chances of making mistakes. Trading without a defined strategy in a volatile environment is dangerous, as the speed of the moves can cause you to lose money quickly. If you find yourself winging it, it is time to walk away, re-evaluate your strategy, and wait for more stable market conditions.

One of the most common mistakes in volatile markets is trading in the hope of recouping losses, which can lead to a vicious cycle of even bigger losses. If you've had a string of losing trades, the temptation to "get even" with the market can be strong, but this behavior rarely pays off. Volatile markets are not the place to try to recoup your losses quickly. Rather than taking on more risk in an already unstable environment, it's better to accept your losses, close your positions, and wait for conditions to improve. If you keep trading just to try to recoup lost money, you'll most likely end up making rash decisions, leading to even more losses.

Another clear sign that it's time to exit a volatile market is when the volatility is excessive relative to your risk tolerance. Every trader has a different level of risk they're willing to take, and volatile markets can test those limits. If price swings are too large for what you can psychologically handle or what your account can handle, it's wise to exit the market before significant losses occur. This doesn't mean you can't trade that market again later, but it's important to recognize when the risk exceeds your ability to manage it. Maintaining firm discipline regarding the amount of risk you're willing to take is crucial to avoiding situations that can irreversibly compromise your capital.

Sometimes, volatility in the market is linked to external events that are difficult to predict or control. Unexpected news, such as a change in a country's economic policies, a financial crisis, or a natural disaster, can trigger an abrupt increase in market volatility. If you find that the market is reacting to events that are beyond your control or your ability to analyze, it is a good time to get out. Trading in an environment where decisions are not based on data or predictable patterns, but on emotional market reactions to unexpected news, significantly increases risk. In these cases, the most sensible thing to do is to wait for the dust to settle and for the market to return to more normal levels of behavior.

Leaving a volatile market is also a valid option when you realize that you don't fully understand what's going on. Volatility can create a chaotic environment where prices seem to move without any apparent logic. If you feel like you can't identify the reasons behind market movements, or if the patterns you used to follow no longer seem to make sense, it's best to take a step back. Trading in a market you don't understand is like driving on a highway without knowing where you're going. Instead of continuing to blindly move forward, it's better to stop, reevaluate the situation, and wait for the market to behave more predictably again.

A good practice is to set clear limits before entering a volatile market. These limits can include a maximum loss threshold you are willing to tolerate or a specific level of volatility you are comfortable trading at. If the market hits any of these limits, you must have the discipline to stick to your plan and get out. Many traders fall into the trap of thinking that "just one more trade" will allow them to recoup their losses or take advantage of a last opportunity. However, staying in a volatile market longer than planned can be a costly mistake. Setting clear limits and sticking to them is an effective way to protect your capital and avoid unnecessary losses.

Finally, one of the most important reasons to leave a volatile market is to protect your emotional and mental well-being. Trading, especially in volatile markets, can be exhausting and stressful. If you find that trading is negatively affecting your mental health, causing anxiety, frustration, or burnout, it's time to stop. Trading under stressful conditions is not only detrimental to your health, but can also lead to poor decision making. Taking a break from the market, even for a short time, can help you regain perspective and come back with a clearer, more focused mind. Sometimes, stepping away from the market is the smartest decision you can make for your well-being and long-term success as a trader.

In short, knowing when to exit a volatile market is a crucial skill for any trader. Whether it's because your emotions are getting the better of you, you're trading without a clear plan, or the volatility is simply too high for your risk tolerance level, it's important to recognize the signs that indicate it's time to get out. Walking away from a volatile market doesn't mean giving up, but rather protecting your capital and your well-being. Remember that there will always be new opportunities in the future and that the most important thing is to preserve your ability to trade when conditions are more favorable. The key to success in the markets is not to trade all the time, but to trade smartly, and sometimes that means knowing when it's best not to trade at all.

The Role of Liquidity in Volatility

Liquidity is a key concept in trading, and its role in volatility is crucial to understanding how markets behave. When we talk about liquidity in financial markets, we are referring to the ease with which an asset can be bought or sold without significantly affecting its price. In other words, a liquid market is one where there are enough buyers and sellers for transactions to be completed quickly and efficiently, with little variation in price. However, when liquidity is low, even small buy or sell orders can lead to large price swings, increasing market volatility.

Imagine you are in a physical market, such as a fruit market. If there are many sellers of apples and many buyers, it is easy to negotiate the price because there is an abundance of apples. You can buy or sell without worrying too much about sudden changes in price. This is similar to a financial market with high liquidity. But if, suddenly, there are only a few sellers of apples left and many people want to buy them, the price can quickly rise due to the scarcity, and negotiations become more difficult. In financial markets, something similar happens when there is low liquidity: prices become more sensitive to transactions and can become unpredictable.

The relationship between liquidity and volatility is fairly straightforward. When there is high liquidity in a market, the price of assets tends to be more stable. This is because there are a large number of buy and sell orders to cushion any sharp movements. For example, if a trader sells a large amount of stock in a liquid market, there are likely to be enough buyers to absorb that sale without causing the price to drop sharply. In contrast, if a trader attempts to sell a significant amount of stock in a market with low liquidity, there may not be enough buyers, which would cause the price to drop sharply.

One reason why liquidity can affect volatility is because in liquid markets, spreads (the difference between the buy price and the sell price) are typically tighter. This means that traders can buy and sell assets without incurring large price differences. In a market with low liquidity, spreads tend to be wider, making it more expensive and complicated to trade as prices can move more drastically from one transaction to the next. For this reason, traders often prefer to trade in liquid markets as it is easier to execute orders without major price surprises.

When liquidity decreases, as is often the case during times of uncertainty or when trading volumes are low, markets become more volatile. This happens because with fewer participants in the market, each transaction has a greater impact on price. A clear example of this can be seen in situations of financial crisis or during unforeseen events, such as surprising economic news or natural disasters. At these times, many traders decide to withdraw from the market, which reduces liquidity and causes prices to become more unstable. Lack of liquidity, combined with fear and uncertainty, can lead to more pronounced and difficult-to-predict price fluctuations.

An interesting aspect of liquidity is that it is not always constant. The liquidity of a market can change throughout the day, depending on a number of factors. For example, in stock markets, liquidity tends to be higher during the hours when major markets, such as those in New York or London, are open. In contrast, during off-peak hours, such as early morning or weekends, liquidity decreases and markets become more volatile. This is an important aspect for traders to consider, as trading during times of low liquidity can mean taking on greater risk due to volatility.

It is also important to consider that liquidity does not affect all assets in the same way. Some assets are, by nature, more liquid than others. For example, stocks of large companies, such as Apple or Microsoft, are highly liquid because there are many buyers and sellers interested in these assets. In contrast, stocks of smaller companies or emerging market stocks tend to be less liquid, making them more susceptible to volatility. Foreign exchange (forex) markets, on the other hand, are typically very liquid due to the huge amount of transactions that take place on a daily basis. However, even in markets as liquid as forex, liquidity can decrease dramatically during major events, such as economic policy announcements or central bank decisions, which increases volatility.

In cryptocurrency markets, liquidity plays an even more critical role. Because it is a relatively new market with fewer participants than other traditional financial markets, liquidity in cryptocurrencies can be more volatile. This means that cryptocurrency prices can change dramatically with very few transactions. In some cases, a single trader with enough capital can influence the price of a cryptocurrency if the market is illiquid. For this reason, volatility in cryptocurrency markets is often much higher compared to other markets, which represents both an opportunity and a risk for traders.

In short, liquidity is one of the most important factors influencing the volatility of a market. The more liquidity there is, the more stable the price of an asset will be and the easier it will be for traders to execute their orders. Conversely, when liquidity is low, prices can become unstable and move unpredictably. Traders need to be aware of the liquidity of the market they are trading in and how it can change based on factors such as the time of day, economic events, or the type of asset they are trading.

Lack of liquidity can be a source of volatility that, if not managed properly, can increase trading risks. That is why understanding the role of liquidity and how it affects volatility is critical to making informed and successful trading decisions.

How to Use Technical Analysis in Volatile Markets

Technical analysis is a fundamental tool for many traders, especially in volatile markets. Through this technique, traders attempt to predict future price movements using charts, patterns, and various mathematical tools. While technical analysis can be useful in any market environment, in a volatile market its importance is amplified. Rapid and large changes in prices make it essential to have a strategy based on the interpretation of objective data, rather than impulsive or emotional decisions. In this chapter, we will look at how to use technical analysis to successfully navigate volatile markets and how this methodology can help you make more informed decisions.

The basic principle of technical analysis is that prices move in patterns that tend to repeat themselves over time. By studying these patterns, traders try to identify entry and exit points in the market. In a volatile market, where prices fluctuate rapidly and sometimes without much apparent logic, technical analysis can provide a structure to make sense of the chaos. Price charts become a map showing the recent history of the market, and technical tools can help find buy or sell signals based on past behavior.

One of the most common tools in technical analysis is moving averages. Moving averages are simply averages of prices calculated over a given time period, such as the last 10, 50, or 200 days. In a volatile market, moving averages help smooth out large fluctuations and identify the overall market trend. If the price is above the moving average, it is a sign that the market is in an uptrend. If it is below it, it suggests a downtrend. Using multiple moving averages together, such as a short-term moving average and a long-term moving average, can help you spot changes in the trend. For example, if a short-term moving average crosses above a long-term moving average, it can be a sign that the trend is changing in an upward direction, which is useful in a volatile environment where changes can be rapid.

Volatility indicators are another key tool in technical analysis when it comes to trading in volatile markets. One of the most popular is the Bollinger Bands indicator. Bollinger Bands consist of a center line (a moving average) and two lines that move away from the average based on recent market volatility. In a volatile market, these bands tend to expand, reflecting an increase in price fluctuation. If an asset's price moves towards the top of the bands, it may be a sign that it is overbought and could be ready for a correction. If it moves towards the lower band, it could be a sign that it is oversold and there could be a buying opportunity. Bollinger Bands allow you to easily visualize how volatility is affecting the market and help you identify potential opportunities.

Another very useful technical indicator in volatile markets is the relative strength index (RSI). The RSI measures the speed and change of price movements, helping to identify whether an asset is overbought or oversold. An RSI above 70 typically indicates that the asset is overbought, while a value below 30 suggests that it is oversold. In a volatile environment, the RSI can move quickly between these extremes, but it is still a valuable tool for identifying points where the market might be exhausting its current trend. For example, if the market has been falling rapidly and the RSI shows that the asset is oversold, you could expect an upward correction shortly.

Chart patterns also play an important role in technical analysis, especially in volatile markets. Patterns such as triangles, flags, and double tops or bottoms can help you anticipate upcoming price movements. An ascending triangle, for example, often indicates that the market is consolidating before a potential breakout to the upside. In volatile markets, these patterns can form quickly, and being familiar with them will allow you to act before the market makes a big move. Additionally, candlestick patterns, such as the hammer or hanging man, are very useful in identifying potential price reversals. In a volatile market, candlesticks can quickly change shape and size, but if you know what to look for, they can provide you with entry or exit signals at just the right time.

It is important to note that in a volatile market, technical analysis should not be used in isolation. Although it provides a wealth of information about past market performance, it is only one part of the equation. Volatile markets are often influenced by external factors such as economic news, political events or unexpected decisions by central banks. These factors are not always immediately reflected on the charts, so it is essential to combine technical analysis with constant monitoring of global news and events.

Another crucial aspect of using technical analysis in volatile markets is risk management. Because price movements can be large and unpredictable, it is essential to use tools such as stop-losses to protect your capital. A stop-loss is an order that is automatically executed when the price of an asset reaches a certain level, helping you limit losses in case the market moves against you. In a volatile market, stop-losses should be placed strategically so that they are not triggered by small movements, but close enough to protect you from large declines. Using technical analysis to identify key levels, such as support and resistance, will allow you to place your stop-losses more effectively.

Discipline is also key when using technical analysis in volatile markets. Because prices can move quickly, it's easy to get caught up in the emotion of the moment and make impulsive decisions. However, technical analysis works best when you follow a clear plan. This means you need to set rules for entering and exiting the market, based on the indicators you're using, and stick to those rules, even when the market becomes chaotic. Volatility can be challenging, but with a disciplined approach based on technical analysis, you can take advantage of opportunities without taking unnecessary risks.

Finally, it is important to remember that technical analysis is not foolproof. No strategy guarantees success in every trade, and in volatile markets, results can be especially unpredictable. The most important thing is to use technical analysis as a tool to reduce uncertainty and make informed decisions, but always being aware that the market has its own rhythm and can sometimes surprise even the most experienced traders.

In short, technical analysis is a powerful tool for trading in volatile markets. By using indicators such as moving averages, Bollinger Bands and RSI, along with chart patterns and good risk management, you can increase your chances of success in a volatile environment. However, the key is discipline and combining technical analysis with a broader understanding of the market context. If you stay focused, avoid impulsive decisions and stick to your trading plan, technical analysis can be your best ally in successfully navigating market volatility.

Volatility in Different Assets

Volatility affects financial markets in different ways, depending on the type of asset being traded. While volatility broadly means fluctuations in prices, each type of asset responds differently to market movements due to its unique characteristics. It is essential to understand how volatility manifests itself in different assets in order to adjust trading strategies and better manage risk. In this chapter, we will explore how volatility varies in assets such as stocks, currencies, bonds, commodities, and cryptocurrencies, and what factors influence their fluctuations.

Let's start with stocks, one of the most popular assets in the financial markets. Stocks represent a stake in a company, and their volatility depends on several factors, such as the company's performance, the state of the broader economy, industry news, and market sentiment. Stocks of large companies with a stable track record are typically less volatile, as they have a more predictable history and are less susceptible to sudden changes. However, stocks of smaller or emerging companies tend to be much more volatile. This is because their smaller size makes them more vulnerable to changes in economic conditions and unexpected events. In addition, news about earnings, changes in company management, or innovations in the industry can lead to rapid movements in the stock price.

Volatility in the stock market can also be affected by external events, such as economic crises, interest rate changes, and government policies. For example, during the COVID-19 pandemic, many stocks experienced extreme volatility due to global uncertainty. Some sectors, such as technology, thrived while others, such as tourism and aviation, suffered dramatic declines. In situations like these, stock prices can experience wild fluctuations, creating both opportunities and risks for traders.

Now let's talk about the foreign exchange market, also known as forex. This is one of the largest and most liquid markets in the world, where currencies are bought and sold in pairs, such as the Euro versus the US Dollar (EUR/USD). Volatility in the foreign exchange market can be very high because prices are influenced by a wide range of global factors, such as monetary policies, interest rates, economic data, and geopolitical events. A single announcement from a central bank, such as an interest rate hike, can trigger large movements in currencies. This is because investors re-evaluate the value of a currency based on its performance compared to other currencies.

Furthermore, the forex market operates 24 hours a day, five days a week, meaning that volatility can occur at any time, depending on where the world's major financial markets are located at the time. For example, during the Asian session, volatility can be lower compared to the opening hours in London and New York, when more transactions take place and more important economic data is released. Still, unexpected events, such as changes in central bank policies or geopolitical tensions, can cause significant movements in currencies. Volatility in forex can offer great opportunities, but it also entails greater risk, as price movements can be rapid and difficult to predict.

Bonds, on the other hand, tend to be less volatile assets compared to stocks and currencies. Bonds represent debt issued by governments or corporations, and their volatility depends primarily on interest rates. When interest rates rise, the value of bonds tends to fall, as investors prefer new bonds that pay higher rates. Conversely, when interest rates fall, existing bonds, which pay a higher rate, become more valuable, and their price rises. In a stable interest rate environment, bonds are usually fairly predictable and less volatile assets.

However, bonds are not completely immune to volatility. During periods of economic uncertainty or when there are concerns about the solvency of a government or company, bonds can experience volatility. This is especially true of emerging market bonds, which are often more volatile due to political and economic uncertainty in those countries. Corporate bonds can also be volatile if the financial situation of the issuing company worsens. However, in general, bonds tend to be viewed as safer and less volatile assets compared to stocks and currencies.

Commodities, such as oil, gold, silver, and wheat, can be highly volatile due to a variety of factors, including supply and demand, weather events, geopolitical conflicts, and changes in government policies. For example, the price of oil is notoriously volatile due to its dependence on factors such as decisions by the Organization of the Petroleum Exporting Countries (OPEC), tensions in oil-producing regions, and fluctuations in global demand. A conflict in an oil-rich region or a decline in production can cause prices to suddenly rise, while an increase in production or an economic slowdown can cause prices to fall.

Gold, on the other hand, is known for being a safe haven asset, meaning it tends to rise in value during times of economic uncertainty. However, it can also be volatile when investors shift their focus to riskier assets in search of higher returns. Agricultural commodities, such as wheat or corn, are volatile due to weather factors and global demand. A drought in a key region can send prices soaring, while a bumper harvest can cause prices to fall.

Finally, cryptocurrencies are perhaps the most volatile assets in today's financial markets. Bitcoin, Ethereum, and other cryptocurrencies have gained popularity in recent years, but their extreme volatility makes them a risky asset class. Cryptocurrency volatility is driven by a combination of factors, such as speculation, news about government regulation, and technological adoption. For example, a single tweet from an influencer or news about regulation in a country can cause huge fluctuations in the price of a cryptocurrency in a matter of minutes. Furthermore, since cryptocurrency markets operate 24 hours a day, movements can occur at any time, making the risk of volatility constant.

In short, volatility in financial markets varies wildly across different assets. Stocks, currencies, bonds, commodities, and cryptocurrencies all have their own volatility dynamics, influenced by specific factors. While some assets, such as bonds, tend to be more stable, others, such as cryptocurrencies, are known for extreme volatility. Understanding how each asset behaves in a volatile environment will allow you to adjust your trading strategies and better manage risk. The key is to tailor your approach based on the asset you are trading and be prepared to handle the ups and downs that accompany volatility in financial markets.

How Information Impacts Markets

Information is one of the most powerful drivers in financial markets. Every day, thousands of news stories, reports, and events affect investors' decisions, and as a result, asset prices in the markets can change abruptly. But why does this happen? How can something as intangible as a news story or a rumor make a stock's price go up or down in a matter of minutes? In this chapter, we'll explore how information impacts markets, how traders use it to make decisions, and why markets often overreact to certain types of news.

When we talk about information, we are referring to all types of data that can influence investors' perception of the future value of an asset. This information can take many forms: economic reports, company announcements, political decisions, changes in regulation, geopolitical tensions or even rumors circulating on social media. All of these can impact investor confidence and, therefore, alter the price of assets.

One of the most influential types of information on markets is economic reports. For example, when a country publishes its unemployment rate or its inflation rate, investors usually react immediately. If the data is better than expected, markets may react positively, as the economy is perceived to be on the right track. Conversely, if the data is worse than anticipated, asset prices may fall, as investors see an uncertain economic future. These reports are closely monitored, and traders are usually ready to act as soon as they are published.

In addition to economic reports, political decisions also have a major impact on markets. For example, if a government announces a change in its fiscal or monetary policies, this can have a direct effect on financial assets. An announcement of a tax increase can cause the shares of certain companies to fall, as investors fear that this will affect their profits. On the other hand, a reduction in interest rates by a central bank can cause markets to react upwards, as investors see that the cost of borrowing is reduced, which is positive for economic growth.

One of the clearest examples of how political information impacts markets is the case of Brexit, when the United Kingdom decided to leave the European Union. Every piece of news about the negotiation process, the possibilities of an agreement or a no-deal exit, caused large movements in the currency market, especially in the pound sterling. The uncertainty surrounding the outcome of the negotiations caused investors to react in an extreme way to any new signal, generating great volatility.

Corporate announcements also play a crucial role in market movements. When a company reports its quarterly results, investors scrutinize every detail: revenue, profits, future projections. If the results are better than expected, the company's stock price can rise rapidly. On the other hand, if the company reports losses or results below expectations, investors may lose confidence and sell their shares, causing the price to fall. The interesting thing is that it's not just what the company reports that matters, but how it compares to market expectations. Even if a company has good results, if it fails to meet investors' high expectations, its price can fall.

In recent years, social media has become an important source of information for investors. Often, rumors or opinions from influential figures can have a significant impact on asset prices. A recent example is the case of cryptocurrencies, where a single tweet from a celebrity or a comment from a famous entrepreneur can cause the price of Bitcoin or Ethereum to skyrocket or crash in a matter of minutes. This shows how, in the age of digital information, non-traditional sources also play an important role in markets.

However, not all information is created equal. Experienced traders know that not all news deserves an immediate reaction. Part of the challenge of trading financial markets is filtering out the useful information from the unhelpful. Often, rumors or misinterpreted news can lead to exaggerated market movements, known as "overreaction." In these cases, asset prices can rise or fall disproportionately to the actual impact of the news. For example, a rumor that a company is launching a new product may cause its stock to rise, but if that product doesn't generate as much interest as expected, the price can quickly correct.

The key to successfully trading in information-driven markets is learning to manage the volatility that information creates. Many traders look for opportunities in the rapid price movements caused by new news. However, it is also crucial to have a clear strategy to avoid getting caught up in the chaos that often surrounds important news. Making impulsive decisions based on unverified information can lead to huge losses.

An important concept in this context is "discounted price." This refers to the idea that all known information is already reflected in the current price of an asset. Most experienced traders do not simply react to the news itself, but to whether that news was already anticipated by the market. If an economic report was already expected and is in line with projections, the market has likely already adjusted prices to reflect that expectation. However, if the news is unexpected or surprising, it can lead to abrupt moves.

Another interesting aspect is how asymmetric information can create opportunities in the market. Asymmetric information occurs when some market participants have access to information before others. Although there are strict regulations to prevent insider trading, in some situations, certain investors may be better informed, giving them a competitive advantage. For example, if an investor has access to more in-depth analysis or is aware of changes in a company's policy before they are made public, they can act early and benefit from volatility.

In short, information is the fuel that drives financial markets. Asset prices are not static; they constantly change in response to new data, announcements, and events that impact investor expectations. The ability to correctly interpret this information, distinguish between what is relevant and what is irrelevant, and act strategically is what distinguishes a successful trader from one who simply goes with the flow of the market. In an environment where information travels at breakneck speed, learning to filter and react appropriately can make the difference between making a profit and suffering a loss in volatile markets.

Coverage and Hedging in Volatile Markets

Hedging and hedging are key terms when we talk about how to protect yourself in volatile markets. For traders and investors, volatility can be both an opportunity and a threat. At times when prices rise and fall unexpectedly, having a hedging strategy can make the difference between preserving capital or quickly losing it. In this chapter, we will explore what hedging is, how it works, and why it is a valuable tool in volatile markets.

When we talk about hedging, we are referring to taking steps to reduce the risk of an investment. In volatile markets, where prices can move drastically in a short period of time, the main objective is to minimize the potential losses that can result from these sudden movements. Hedging does not seek to completely eliminate risk, but rather to limit it. Imagine that hedging is like insurance: you pay a premium to protect yourself against an unwanted event. If that event occurs, the insurance covers you, at least in part, for the losses you might have suffered.

One of the most common ways to hedge is by using financial derivatives, such as options or futures. Derivatives are contracts whose value depends on the price of another asset, such as a stock, currency, or commodity. For example, if you own shares of a company and you fear that its price may fall, you might buy a put option. This option gives you the right, but not the obligation, to sell your shares at a predetermined price. If the stock price falls, the option will allow you to sell them at a higher than market price, offsetting some of your losses.

Another popular hedging strategy is the use of futures contracts. A futures contract is an agreement to buy or sell an asset at a specific price on a future date. In volatile markets, futures contracts are often used to protect against sharp changes in the prices of commodities such as oil, gold, or wheat. If you are a wheat farmer and you fear that the price of wheat will fall in the coming months, you can sell a futures contract. This way, you secure a fixed price for your output, regardless of how the market behaves in the future. If the price of wheat falls, you have avoided losing money, since you have already locked in the price at a higher level. However, if the price rises, you will not be able to profit from the increase because you had already agreed to sell at a lower price. This is the nature of hedging: you protect your investments, but you also give up some potential gains.

Hedging is especially useful for companies that rely on raw materials or are exposed to fluctuations in exchange rates. For example, an airline that purchases large amounts of fuel may want to protect itself against a potential rise in oil prices. By using futures contracts, the airline can lock in a fixed price for fuel, allowing it to better plan its operating costs without having to worry about market ups and downs. Similarly, a company that imports products from abroad could use hedging to protect itself against fluctuations in exchange rates. If the value of the foreign currency rises, the hedge will protect the company from paying more for its imported products.

However, it's not just large companies that can benefit from hedging. Individual traders can also use these strategies to protect their investments. Imagine you've invested in a portfolio of stocks and the markets become extremely volatile. Instead of selling your shares, you could use put options or futures contracts to reduce your risk exposure. This allows you to hold onto your investment for the long term while protecting yourself from potential short-term losses. Sure, the cost of hedging can eat into your profits, but for many investors, the peace of mind that comes from knowing they're protected is worth it.

Besides derivatives, there are also other methods of hedging. One of them is to diversify your investment portfolio. Diversification involves investing in different types of assets, such as stocks, bonds, real estate, or even cryptocurrencies. The idea behind diversification is that when one asset loses value, another might be gaining. For example, in times of volatility in the stock market, bonds or gold tend to be considered safer assets. By having a diversified portfolio, you reduce the impact of volatility on a single sector or type of asset. This way, if a particular market crashes, your losses will be partially offset by assets that have maintained or increased their value.

Another common hedging approach is investing in safe haven assets. Safe haven assets are those that tend to maintain their value, or even increase, in times of uncertainty and volatility. Gold is one of the most well-known examples. When markets become unstable, many investors turn to gold as a way to protect their wealth. Gold has historically been seen as a store of value, and its price tends to rise when other assets, such as stocks, lose value. Other examples of safe haven assets include the US dollar and US Treasury bonds, which are also often in demand in times of crisis.

However, it is important to note that hedging is not a perfect strategy. As we mentioned earlier, hedging comes at a cost. If you decide to buy an option or futures contract to protect yourself against volatility, you will be paying a premium or giving up potential gains. This means that in some cases, if the market does not move as you expected, you could end up losing more money than you would have without hedging. That is why it is crucial that traders and investors use hedging carefully and with a clear strategy in mind.

Hedging also requires a solid understanding of the financial instruments you are going to use. It is not a technique that should be taken lightly, as misuse of hedging can lead to more complications than solutions. For example, if you use derivatives without fully understanding how they work, you could end up incurring unnecessary costs or taking risks you had not planned for. Therefore, for those who want to implement hedging strategies in their portfolios, it is important to educate yourself well or have the support of a specialized financial advisor.

In short, hedging and hedging are essential tools for protecting yourself in volatile markets. While they do not completely eliminate risk, they can help minimize losses and offer greater peace of mind in times of uncertainty. Both large investors and individual traders can benefit from using hedging strategies, as long as they understand the associated costs and risks. In a world where markets can change at the drop of a hat, being prepared for the unexpected is key, and hedging offers just that protection.

Creating a Trading Plan in Volatile Markets

Creating a trading plan is one of the most important things any trader, whether beginner or experienced, should do before trading in volatile markets. A volatile market can be exciting and full of opportunities, but it can also be unpredictable and dangerous if you don't have a clear strategy. The goal of a trading plan is to provide a roadmap for making informed decisions and avoiding impulsive or emotional decisions that can often lead to significant losses.

The first step in creating a trading plan in volatile markets is to define your goals. It's important to know what you hope to achieve with your trades. Are you looking for short-term gains or do you prefer a more long-term strategy? What is your risk tolerance? Volatile markets can offer great opportunities, but they also come with a high level of risk. Having a clear idea of your goals and the level of risk you are willing to take will help you stay focused and avoid deviating from your strategy.

Once you've set your goals, the next step is to identify the assets you want to trade. Not all assets behave the same in volatile markets. Some assets, such as cryptocurrencies or technology stocks, can experience sharp, rapid movements, while others, such as bonds or shares of more stable companies, tend to be less volatile. It's critical that you choose assets that align with your risk tolerance and goals. Additionally, it's advisable to diversify your portfolio, which means trading in different types of assets to reduce the impact of volatility in a single market.

A crucial part of your trading plan in volatile markets is defining your entry and exit points. Volatility can cause asset prices to rise and fall rapidly, which can create both opportunities and risks. Before entering a trade, you should be clear about what price you would be willing to buy at and what price you would be willing to sell at. These entry and exit points should be based on technical or fundamental analysis and not on emotion or impulse. Defining these levels beforehand will help you avoid making hasty decisions during times of high volatility.

Using stop-loss orders is a key tool in a trading plan for volatile markets. A stop-loss is an order that is automatically placed when the price of an asset reaches a certain level, selling or buying to limit your losses. In a volatile environment, prices can quickly move in the opposite direction than you expected, and a stop-loss will protect you from larger losses than you could bear. While it can be tempting to let a trade continue in the hope that the market will turn in your favor, a stop-loss ensures that you don't lose more than you are willing to lose. Defining stop-loss levels before entering a trade is essential to effectively managing risk.

In addition to stop-loss orders, it is also important to use take-profit orders. These orders are automatically triggered when the price of an asset reaches a predetermined profit level. In volatile markets, where prices can fluctuate rapidly and abruptly, having a clear strategy for taking profits is crucial. If you do not have a clear plan for when to take your profits, you could miss the opportunity to close a trade for a profit before the market takes an unexpected turn. As with stop-loss orders, take-profit orders allow you to execute your trading plan in a more disciplined manner and without getting carried away by the emotion of the moment.

Technical analysis is another essential tool in a trading plan for volatile markets. Through charts, patterns, and different technical indicators, you can identify trends and potential entry or exit points in the market. Tools such as moving averages, relative strength index (RSI), or Bollinger bands will help you spot when an asset is overbought or oversold, or when a correction is likely to occur. In volatile markets, where prices can move in large ranges in short periods of time, technical analysis can give you an edge in making informed, data-driven decisions, rather than reacting to sudden market movements.

However, technical analysis is not everything. In a trading plan, it is also important to pay attention to fundamental analysis, especially in volatile markets. Fundamental analysis focuses on the underlying economic and financial factors that can influence the value of an asset. For example, if you are trading stocks, you should analyze the company's revenue, profits, debt, and market position. If you are trading currencies, you should keep a close eye on central bank policies, economic data, and geopolitical events. While volatility can be driven by short-term movements, economic fundamentals tend to influence long-term price movements.

Risk management is another crucial component of your trading plan. In volatile markets, it's easy to get carried away by excitement or panic, but it's vital to set clear limits on how much capital you're willing to risk on each trade. A general rule of thumb in trading is to risk no more than 1-2% of your total capital on a single trade. This way, if things don't go your way, your losses will be limited and you won't jeopardize your entire portfolio. In a volatile environment, risk management becomes even more important, as price fluctuations can be more extreme and faster.

Another important element of a trading plan is time. You need to decide how much time you are willing to spend on each trade. In volatile markets, prices can change dramatically in a matter of minutes or hours, so if you are trading short-term, you need to be willing to monitor the markets constantly. On the other hand, if you have a longer-term strategy, such as investing in a company that you believe has good fundamentals, you will need to be patient and not be swayed by daily market fluctuations. Defining a time frame for each trade will help you maintain discipline and avoid impulsive decisions.

Trading psychology also plays a big role in creating a trading plan, especially in volatile markets. Volatility can create an emotional rollercoaster for traders, and it's easy to fall into the trap of acting out of fear or greed. Fear can cause you to close a trade too early, while greed can cause you to hold onto a position for longer than necessary, in the hope of making more profit. To combat this, it's essential to have a clear plan and stick to it, regardless of what the market is doing. A well-thought-out plan will give you the confidence to make decisions based on logic and not emotion.

It's important to review and adjust your trading plan regularly. Markets change, and what worked in one environment may not work in another. If you notice that certain aspects of your strategy aren't producing the results you expected, it's crucial to make adjustments. This doesn't mean you should change your plan every time you suffer a loss, but you should be willing to adapt to new market conditions. Sometimes the market may become more volatile than you anticipated, or perhaps the tools you're using are no longer as effective. Reviewing your plan with an open mind will allow you to evolve as a trader and improve your results in the long run.

In short, creating a trading plan in volatile markets is an essential step for any trader looking to succeed in an unpredictable environment. A clear plan helps you make more informed decisions, manage risk effectively, and stay focused on your goals. In volatile markets, where price movements can be rapid and extreme, having a well-defined strategy is the key to trading with confidence and avoiding impulsive decisions that could lead to big losses.

www.ingramcontent.com/pod-product-compliance
Lightning Source LLC
Chambersburg PA
CBHW051852130726
47987CB00002B/801